DANCING WITH THE MIDWIVES

DANCING WITH THE MIDWIVES

ANN FAISON

BLACK DRAGONFLY BOOKS

Black Dragonfly Books
936 E Elizabeth St
Pasadena CA 91104

dancingwiththemidwives.com

Interior design by Elinor Nissley, revised by Bill Smith
Cover design by Bill Smith, designSimple.com
Back cover photo by Darcy Hemley, DarcyHemley.com

Cover and interior drawings by the author

Printed in the U.S.

Thanks to Simon Warwick-Smith, Bill Smith, Elinor Nissley, Laurence Dumortier, Chris Napolitano, Jodi Wille, David Elliott and the writer's group, and the many readers and co-editors who helped me write this book.
Special thanks to Dave, Grace and Frances.

Dancing with the Midwives is typeset using Hoefler Text (10pts on 18pts body text) and Scala Sans.

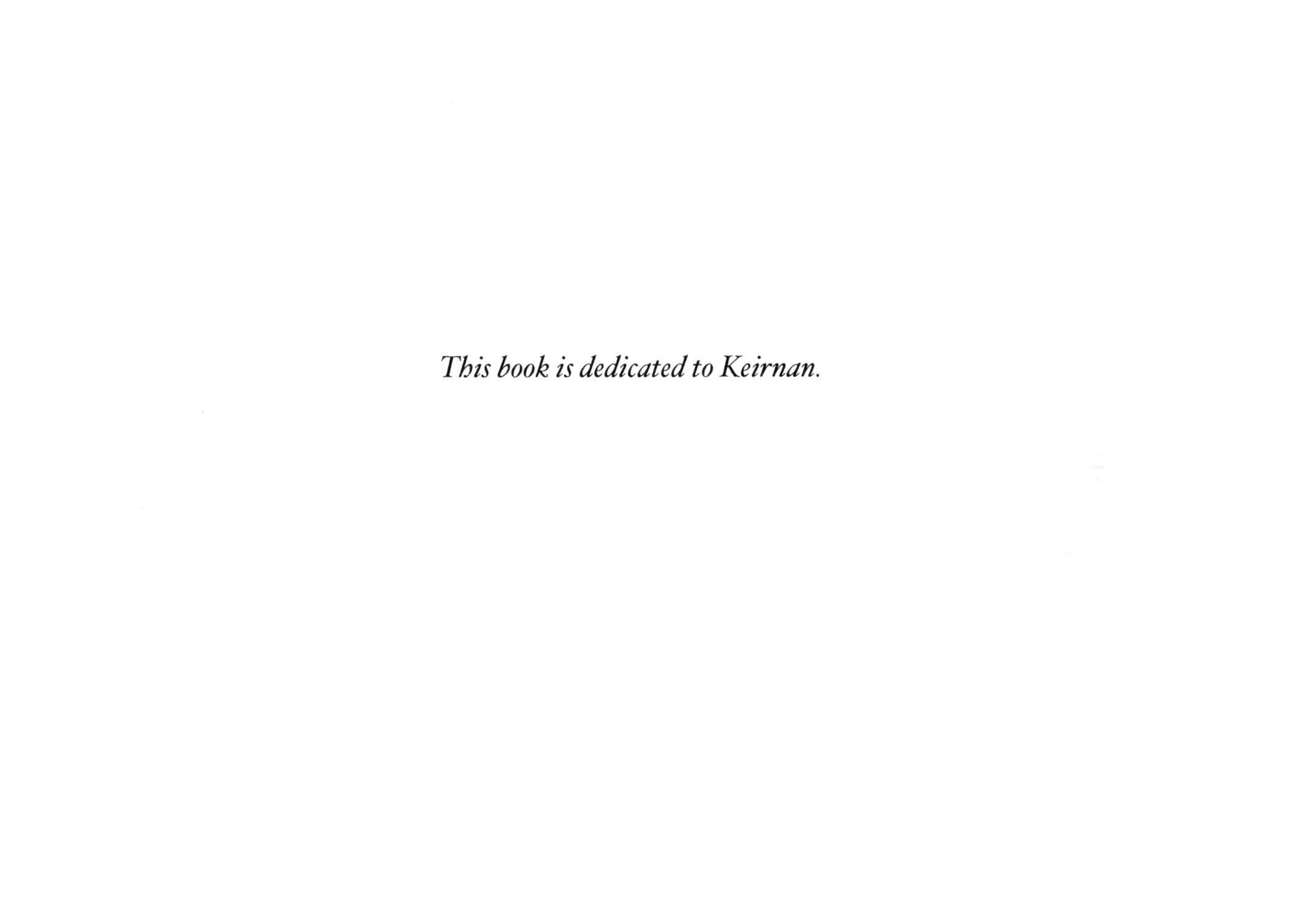

This book is dedicated to Keirnan.

Contents

Drawings

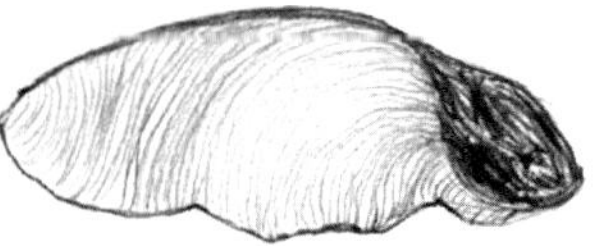

A Story I Like to Tell.

I have been telling this story for some time, and it has changed, and it has changed me, and we are both growing like an old tree, deeper and broader still. It begins with the sudden discovery that a pregnancy six months along has ended in death. It begins with the birth of the dead baby.

This is a story of transformation, brought about by birth and death being bound up together, and leaving in their wake no vessel for the stream of love both had created. I write of a mother's love, but a father's and a sister's too, for their grief was inextricably linked with mine, expanding all of us at once. I speak of change, and how this short life forced it on us fast, making it impossible to remember who we were before she came.

I was no stranger to grief. My mother died when I was still young and I entered adulthood through dark doors, missing her and mourning my own innocence. I always appreciated my early experience and what I learned from it, but never was I more grateful than when faced with the death of my own child. My history was like an old friend who helped me appreciate the landscape of this new experience as it passed.

We named our baby Keirnan, and she is part of our family. It's not that we think or talk about her constantly, though we did at first, but her absence is more of a presence, and time proves that presence to be sustaining. So this is a story I like to tell, and the telling of it is nourishing for me.

Ceremony

We tried to have another one of our ceremonies for Keirnan tonight. I brought out candles, treats and the few mementos we have. I started to say something but it felt flat and forced. I didn't feel like being the ringleader again, so I didn't say anything for a while. I thought, Maybe this time we can just be in this space and not do anything. But not doing anything didn't satisfy me. Grace was busy entertaining us with stories and songs and eventually I rose to clean up. A little while later Dave seemed irritated.
Can I blow out the candles? He asked.

I asked him what he wanted. He said the rituals needed more structure, something to hold onto. That's just it, I bawled. There is nothing. No stories, no images in our minds of our daughter and yet she lived and we love her and we miss her. We miss being excited about her.

Grace is putting flower petals on my legs. One by one she places them, working carefully, in long rows. They are large and white and beginning to brown. We collected them today at the botanical gardens. They were covering the ground under a tree like a carpet of love. She is working her way up my arms so that I can't move. Lie down, she demands, so I can do your face.

Ladybug

A ladybug lands on a breezy blue sky day under a canopy of Oaks. She is crawling down my sleeve when I notice something is wrong with her. Time stops and waits for me to realize that a deformed ladybug has found me. Her right side looks like a wrecked car. Instead of a bright shell for her wing there is a mangled mass that looks as if it were melted by a match into a hard black ball. The wing protrudes at a right angle, useless. The left side is perfect, the wing neatly encased in a shell that is light orange with tiny black spots. Her legs work fine and when she flutters her single wing, it turns her body in a tight circle. I study her, trying to determine what happened and decide it must be something she was born with. She is used to it. She scurries along like a normal ladybug, then spins a little donut on my book.

Conversation

The new person cutting my hair asks if we plan to have more kids and something allows me to say no, we had three, and one died. That's enough. The scissors don't stop and instead of apologizing she asks questions. I think, That's what I do when someone tells me their mother died. She asks, How did she die? How long was she alive? Was she born? The last one is unusual but I answer anyway. Her interest and ease in the conversation give her away. When she was six or seven she had a sister who lived two days. She remembers going to the hospital and seeing her alive. She says her little sister is a big part of her life and shows me where she has her sister's name tattooed on her arm. When she was little she would write notes to her sister, tie them to balloons and send them up.

Dance

Grace spent two nights with her babysitter Yoly so I could rest after Keirnan's birth. Grace knew what had happened. We were all in the room when the ultrasound showed that there was no heartbeat. Minutes later I had kissed her soft round face in the dark parking structure of the hospital as Dave strapped her into her car seat, and said goodbye.

When Yoly brought her home two days later it felt as though we had not seen each other for weeks. Dave had gone to pick up dinner so we were alone in the house. I was in my nightgown. She requested her current favorite song with the lilting girlish voice singing over a watery harp, and we started to dance. We held hands and twirled around,

slowly at first, then faster until we were laughing, almost crying. She was all lit up and excited by my uncharacteristic lack of things to do and our fast dancing. We were thrilled to be together. Our faces made one big smile that carried us out of the house, over the trees, looking down on all the birds in their branches.

Mummy

I am holding a dead baby crow
Not in my hands,
It is in a box
On my desk

Found on a walk today
Dave recognized it
I thought it was part of a tree

Like a twisted root
Its body curled
As if it never left the egg

I thought I might try
To make a drawing
But I can't
I can barely open the box

It makes my heart jump
My breath harden
Because it is half skeleton
Half mummy

Half born
Half dead
Half beautiful
Half hideous

I need to bury it
Like I need to bury
The placenta
And the ashes

Large head and long beak
On the skull a tiny pattern
Runs down the center
Like a braid

Threshold

The doctor said she had been dead for a week or ten days, but when precisely did she go? She slipped silently into death, inside me. Was I on the plane to San Francisco with Grace? Were we watching the ice skaters in the park? So many moments I don't remember over that time. Doing the dishes, taking out the garbage, talking on the phone, getting Grace dressed, putting her to bed. All the things I do in a day and don't remember. When I try to imagine the time that passed in that period, the in between moments, they are blurred together and washed in white. The times I do remember stand out like little pictures: Riding the merry-go-round with Dad and Sally, watching Grace walk along a wall holding Dave's hand, holding her body while she cried in pain, dressed only in a diaper, in the hotel room. We were doing all that. I was doing something, sleeping maybe, when Keirnan passed away.

Snowstorm

I was born during a snow storm
The famous blizzard of '64
They said the cab almost didn't make it
There in time

They would tell me much later that we were close
That she took me everywhere
That I was her baby
And I have pictures that show it that way

But my memory is different
In the pictures I draw

There is a gaping wound
A missing limb

I choose to forget
All that we did together
How she taught me to sew and to cook
And gave me good advice about my body

I remember her hands
Soft and veiny
Taken for granted crossing streets
Hard to let go of at night

She didn't leave a lot
Some shirts and sweaters

Photographs she took and darkroom equipment
A wedding band I wore until I lost it

Once
When I was lost in my twenties
She came back to me in a dream
A snowstorm

Me rushing outside in pajamas and bare feet
Running on the snow covered sidewalk to catch up
She not stopping and acting surprised
My desperation and all my questions

All she says with a half smile is
You're doing fine

The message is sweet
Her delivery cold

I always wanted that missed moment
Like I imagined others had
When a mother tells her daughter
She will be loved forever

I see her full of love
And sorrow, which she hid well
I can still hear her whooping laughter
Floating down the elevator shaft

Womb Chair

Sitting here in the Womb Chair, I am listening to music with a fire burning in the fireplace. Dave got a big supply of firewood the other day. He said he wanted to enjoy this house more. I decided that when all these flowers die, I will ask him to get more. I want to always keep flowers in the house.

Death makes us slow down. All the rushing about we were doing is fizzled to nothing. There is nothing to do. Nothing to get done except what we feel like doing. Like a vacation.

I can just sit. Enjoy my beautiful daughter. My sweet husband. My grumpy cat. This old chair. The sound of the fire. The smell of the breeze through the window.

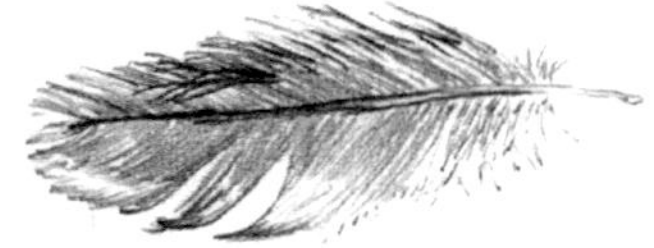

Desert Drive

The tattoos, motorcycles, metal, large hoop earrings framing bald heads, the beans, the bones, all the black, the dusty, the worn, the rough, the badly arranged and poorly executed, the dirt roads, the grit, the glare and the relentless wind. It all feels like death. It's the aesthetic of being cozy with things dead, or dying. It says, everything has to fight to survive here.

I took myself away for the weekend and I'm not sure Dave really understood. We are processing this differently, each at our own pace. I need to dive in to the dark, while he seems to let it wash over him, slowly. I know Grace needs me too, but if I don't take care of myself what good am I to them? I drove to the desert for all of its empty space. And the full moon. I brought notebooks to write in and high expectations of breaking through the hardened emotional shell that wants to grow around me. Upon entering the town where I'll be staying, I spot a portable billboard with letters clinging to rusted wires that reads:

Life here is a test. Heaven and hell are waiting.

A young girl strikingly put together from the thrift store down the road glides through the café where I sit with my books and pens. She has two phones. She seems slightly uneasy dressed that way out here in the sandy gloom where everyone is in dusted jeans or army fatigues, but also enjoying it a little. It helps her float. She notices me and smiles which warms my heart instantly. Her name is Autumn.

It would be easy to stay here. Easy to sink into desert life for a while. Last night I lay on a recliner behind my hotel room, under the stars. I listened to desert sounds and drank up desert air, hoping for something. A shift. An opening. A release of some kind. Mostly I felt numb from all the tears.

Lots of tourists out here. Lots of far flung dust encrusted plates on SUV's and campers too fancy for locals. Climbers act like they live here, and maybe they do. I don't think I could. Everyone's hair is stringy from the dusty wind. Truth is, the shell might need to get harder before it can soften.

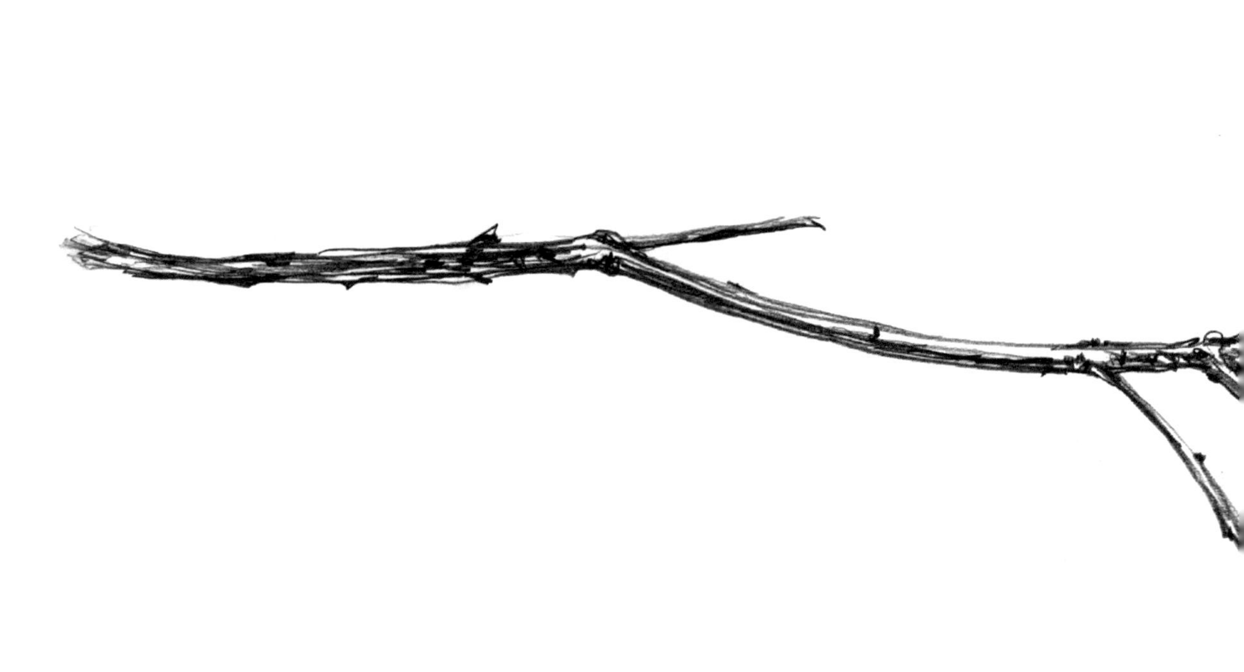

Katherine

My love,

Thanks for all your love. It means so much to me.

I want to tell you something that I don't quite have the courage to tell most, but I know you will understand: I don't like hearing the word "sorry" anymore. Usually when people say it to me my response is "I know you are" which helps me to deflect it back to the person saying it while acknowledging the sentiment. The reason I don't like it is because I'm *not* sorry. And that's because I believe Keirnan's life was simply that. Her life. I don't yet understand why she spent just six months in this family, but I hope to. There is so much to learn from all of this, about her, and of course about ourselves. I look forward to all of it.

Visit

I went to go see Laura's baby. I held him and my breath at the same time. When I left I felt myself disintegrating. Holding him felt bad. Like I didn't remember how. Holding him felt bad. Like I may never get the chance to know again. He wasn't mine. I want to be okay with holding a newborn, but I'm not. I want to be okay with seeing pregnant women, but I'm not. I want to be beyond jealousy and desire and pettiness, but I'm not. All I can do is catch myself, and let go.

Interview

I am putting Grace down for her nap when she asks me, *Where did the baby go?* You mean Keirnan? I answer, practicing the new name. *Is Keirnan my sister?* Yes. *Is she still coming?* No, Grace, she died and she can't come anymore. She is somewhere else now. *Where?* I don't know. No one knows what happens when we die. But we can imagine her up in the sky if we want to. *Can I visit her up there?* She asks, clearly not needing her imagination to put Keirnan in the sky. Maybe you can, I say. Maybe in your dreams or in your heart, you can visit with her. You can always talk to her. *Will she listen?* Yes. She will listen.

My sister Sally sent us a book called *I am a Big Sister*. It's the kind that tells the story of the new sibling being born and is designed to help the older child cope with all the changes.

There were a lot of blank spaces to write your child's name, add pictures and other details. Sally had pasted a picture of Grace into the little frame on the cover and it made me upset to look at it. I think more than anything I wanted a sibling for Grace. I grew up with three and always enjoyed my friendships with them, especially Sally who is closest to me in age. I had my heart set on having two children close together because I thought it would make them good friends later. But the shape of our family is not up to me.

Grace is playing with her little stuffed green frog, talking to him about how he has to take his nap. Any other questions? I ask, not ready for her to be finished with our conversation. Answering her questions is reassuring. *Do you love Keirnan?* She asks looking at her frog's face. Yes, very much, and sometimes that is hard. *Why?* Her face turns to mine, demanding an explanation. Well, just because she is not here. It makes me miss her. *I don't miss her*, Grace says with certainty. *I'm going to talk to her. I am a big sister now.*

Tree

I am sitting here, blocking traffic on a tree that is lying down alive. Its trunk grows horizontally out of the ground, long enough for two people to lie outstretched, before it turns reaching its leafy branches skyward. The tree has generously made a perfect seat for me and the ants are piling up on either side of my thighs, reminding me how easy it is to create chaos. Ants are clearly adaptable, but like us, need order. When order is ruptured they run in circles, looking very stressed.

There is no knowing Keirnan. There is buzzing. There is a bee, a crow crowing. But there is no message waiting for me. There are lessons, unfolding. Like caring for myself.

People can say, Take care of yourself! until they are blue in the face and we don't do it. Especially mothers. Not until we are forced with our faces in the mud.

The tree is not fazed by my weight. Trees are sentinels, standing still, not bothering with anyone, but more alive. The one I'm on is unique because I can feel it move. When I let my feet dangle, I can't feel the sway. But when I stand on the ground and lean against the trunk, I can feel the movement, barely perceptible, just enough to make me feel slightly dizzy. It's precious, this gentle bumping against me, like a baby turning inside.

Post Partum

The first few days were full of extremes. I had moments, sometime hours, when I felt utterly connected to everything around me and excited just to be alive. I was like a butterfly, fluttering through the house, oblivious to the mundane, noticing only colors and shapes. Other times I was a lead balloon, dragging my bloated body out from the dark bedroom down the long hallway to the florescent green of the bathroom. I was useless, inert.

Now I have good days and bad days. Good days are when I feel almost normal, like I can function, and bad days are when I am a raw nerve unable to get out of bed. Ironically, I feel more at home on the bad days. Sadness and tears and the hollow feeling in my chest are all familiar, comforting and honest. I feel I am doing something even when all I do is sleep and stare.

On a so-called good day, I imagine my heart is resting. The sun shines and beckons. But I feel I am cheating. Abandoning her. I am not supposed to feel normal. Or normal does not feel normal. Bad feels normal and normal feels bad.

Spain

What is it I feel
Or don't
Holding her
Limp body

Barely breathing
Dead with sleep
Over a strange crib
In Spain

I feel her warmth
And weight
Her sweet smelling silken flesh
Pressing into mine

I check my heart
Finding only air
The dead space
Of a dark cavern

Ashes

I remember my father struggling to open the box my mother arrived in. He used a kitchen can opener for the aluminum container inside. Dad carefully poured her ashes into a hole dug into the ground at the cemetery. A small crab apple tree was planted on top.

What to do with the ashes. We still have Keirnan's. It was my first trip out of the house when we picked them up at the mortuary two weeks after she was born. We were given two options for the vessel that would hold her, neither of which satisfied us. The undertaker explained that she would only fill something the size of a salt shaker and I couldn't stop the thought of shaking her ashes over a plate of spaghetti. He led us to a room where the fancy urns were displayed. They were all the size of a cookie jar, and some had smaller matching "keepsake" urns tucked behind them that were about saltshaker size. We agreed immediately on the one we wanted. It was brass and had a lovely pot-bellied shape with cream colored stones decorating the base and midriff.

We knew we would have to hide the pretty little urn from Grace. She would have wanted to play with it and that would have broken our hearts. So Dave kept it on a shelf in his studio, which was under the house. One night he told me he liked having her down there with him. He said he felt sad that he never held her body. You held her for six months, he cried.

A few days later I spotted a tiny silver bottle in an antique mall while Dave was across the street in a record store. It was shaped like a heart with a flat bottom and hung on an awkward chain. I took it to a jewelry maker friend who put Keirnan's birthstone on its little round top, a silver letter K on the front side and gave it a new chain. One night while Dave slept upstairs, I carefully put some of Keirnan's ashes into the miniature bottle using the tiny spoon that came inside it. The next morning I gave it to him for Father's Day.

He wore it every day for about a year, tucked under his shirt. He's not a jewelry person so eventually the necklace migrated to his bag where he still carries it today. The urn with the rest of her ashes lives on top of his dresser, in a box, slightly buried under snapshots and wild colorful drawings the kids have made. When we planted some trees in the backyard this past fall I suggested we might bury the ashes, thinking of my mother under the crab apple. But Dave just gave me the look he gives whenever he is simply not up for a discussion. I knew he was right. We buried my mother's ashes a couple of years after she died, when we felt it was time. It's not the same with a baby. And like Dave, I still want to hold her.

Dear Mom

The house on Long Island is entirely different but I'm sure you knew that. It's been this way for at least fifteen years. The sky lights, the modern but smaller kitchen, the glass doors all along the side of the house that faces the bay. It's much lighter and more open than it was. I might have done the same thing but I still greet the renovation as a kind of betrayal. Somehow I miss all the small dark rooms that let me hide or play by myself without anyone wondering where I was. There is a new feeling to it all, covering up the history, as if it was something to hide.

The porch is almost the same except for the white wicker chairs that replaced the old wooden ones I scratched my name into when I was five and the cement floor is grey now instead of the brick red you painted it. I remember painting it with you. You let me hold the brush and try the roller, unconcerned I guess that it be perfect.

Some things don't change. Like the way the air feels at night. It hit me as we got out of our air-conditioned rental car with our suitcases. It is heavy and sits on you. The night sky is full of stars and the sound of crickets. The creak of the annex door is exactly the same, and the strong mildew smell inside. It smells of childhood. The papery walls and the pine trim seem to exhale it. In all the seasons of all the years I have been coming here it has never changed. I am sure it was the same when you were a girl. The carved wooden panels sent back from Japan along with the wide straw hats and the rice paper sliding doors which, as you can imagine, are all falling apart. Even the poster of the busy harbor with HONG KONG in big letters across the top is still hanging there. I know you loved hiding out in the annex too. It's the place where I still feel you the most.

Neighbors

She drives up in her big beige minivan that is crunched in on one side. She climbs slowly out and walks up the steps to the front door in housewife jeans and a large white tee shirt, keys dangling on a long tether, multiple plastic bags in each hand. She pauses for a second at the top of the steps, taking in the view of the hills, then opens the front door. Her head is bowed but she looks better, more alive then she has.

The front lawn is lined with roses that are pink, red, orange and white. The house looks more active than it did when we delivered cookies, two weeks earlier. That day there had been a big black ribbon tied to the railing, leftover from a large gathering the previous week. We wondered what it was and then heard from a neighbor that a young girl had been killed at school. A gunshot to her chest. When we knocked, her teenage brother opened the door. They told you? he asked, incredulous, the way young people are when someone they love dies. His father, a short, gray haired but sturdy man came up behind him. He pulled us inside to see her picture, which he lifted down from its place surrounded by flowers on the mantle. She was young but already beautiful. Long thick black hair fell behind her full adolescent face. Sparkling eyes looked right at me. Teeth with braces gleamed and her father beamed as he told us her name. All I could think to say was, She is beautiful. Tears streaming.

A few white plastic chairs still lined the periphery of the living room. Stacks of them stood outside on the little front porch. The back of the house was dark and heavy with the mother's presence, her grief trumping that of the others. I couldn't remember ever having seen her. I guessed she had not emerged from her room since the wake.

The first time I saw the mother, she was sitting on the front porch with a blanket over her lap. She looked fragile and disoriented. Her grief was boundless and reaching out to the surrounding hills and houses. Our house. Since then, I have watched her take steps out: Following her small son out to the ice cream truck, his bouncy energy highlighting her wilted posture, and solemnly paying the man, without her son's happiness touching her. Now, she is carrying groceries, making multiple trips from the van to the house. She looks more stable.

Every day I stare at their house from my kitchen window. It stares back. It stands out among the ugly houses that surround it in a way that it never did before. It seems to glow. I can't imagine the inside, even having glimpsed it. How will the family recover from the death of a child on the edge of adulthood? The only girl. It seems so unfair. A stillborn baby.

As she makes her third trip from the van to the house, I contemplate running out to introduce myself. I want to tell her I lost my daughter too. I feel guilty, like a little girl, spying on her. I want her to know I am thinking of her, receiving her grief as part of my own. I want her to know I too am unstable. Unable to put it all back together, still. I want to sit on her couch, hold her hand and cry. Together.

But I don't move. Instead I stare. Her daughter was full grown and mine was barely formed. She must be suffering more than I, she must know things I don't know. I cannot help her. The language barrier, the cultural and religious barriers all stand strong and tall. But I want to help. I am drawn to her. Maybe I think she can help me.

Summer House

A dog's barking ripples through me
The sharp cracks penetrate my skin, the flesh and bones
Am I?
Flesh and bone?
Or am I something else?
More
Am I water or jelly or something like
Rubber?
Am I one thing, not all these separate parts
Am I a boat, riding
On silent currents

Or a bird
Doing the same?

The screen door slams
Its particular series of sound brings up girlhood summers
Running with sandy feet across these floors
the grass
the splintery boardwalk
Even the mosquitoes are part of this place
Their night time buzzing enough to drive a child insane

So many things here stuck in memory forever
Locked up
Only to be opened by returning
by hearing, smelling, then feeling them again
Hot sand at the beach
Riding the ferry
Diesel fumes confused with sea air
Salty skin and sticky heat

The volunteer Fire Department siren at noon
The train in the evening
And at dawn the sounds of these birds, unheard elsewhere,
unidentified by name
A screechy metallic song first
The whistley ho hum of another
and the twit twit twittering of hundreds of others
flung over all of it like a blanket on top

What does it conjure besides pictures and sensations?
Is it love? And is that what I am?

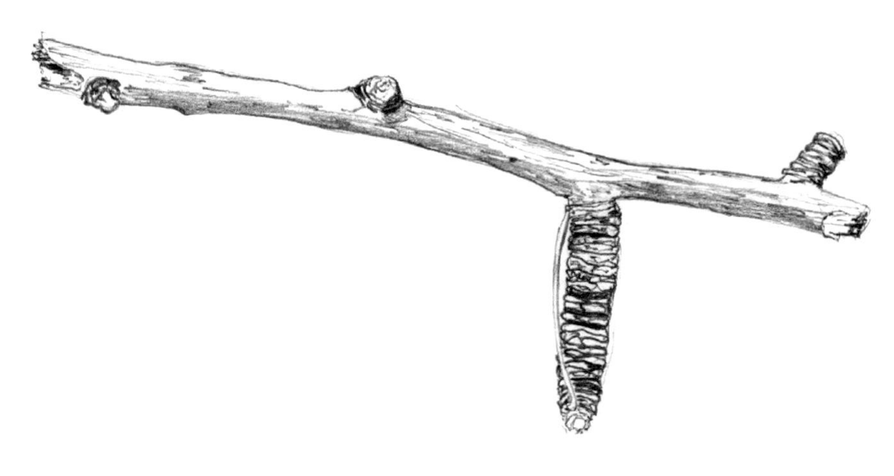

Dancing with the Midwives

I am not finished. Not ready. My belly like a balloon. A hospital room. Lights and monitors and pain in my gut. I feel fear like a deep wound within me. Men and women stand around my bed, waiting. I am not waiting. I feel trapped like a bear, metal teeth biting my paw.

The doctor gave us the bad news. On the outside I act the good girl, cooperating, but inside I dream of the woods and of letting this body come out in its own time and in its own way without drugs or nurses or cold hard floors. I break the trap. I run up in my mind and disappear to a place where all the women are midwives. Where they embrace me and make a space for me to have this baby in their care.

They feed me vegetable soup and let me crawl around on all fours and into a pit in the earth, if I want to and I do. Yes I do. And they smile and even laugh while they light candles to honor her and to bring forth her spirit, which will help bring forth her remains. Really it's up to me to release her, and they understand this and I am beginning to. I dig deeper into the rich brown dirt with my hands and let go a little with my heart. They give me the gift of patience and it pays. First a foot and they all clap and laugh and we tell jokes about ugly feet and her spirit understands we mean no disrespect. Another contraction pushes out more flesh. It is lumpy and hard to discern what is what and no one cares but me. I still want a baby. Something whole. I am still lying in the pit and they are dancing around me in a joyful chant until I get up and join them hoping gravity will work her magic. Bring the body to earth. The corpse inside me is laid bare. It is hanging from my bottom, her head still inside but I join the circle anyway and these women don't care. They have seen it all and they are not disgusted. They are not even sad. They are dancing around me like a God.

I open my eyes to florescent lighting, pea green walls and a circle of faces staring at what I can only feel. Nurses, the doctor, Margo and Dave, everyone is sad to see a dead baby, half born. I can't see anything. I am floating high above. I am dancing with the midwives. I am chanting and singing with her spirit up high. I am celebrating her birth. I don't understand their somber expressions and they don't even notice my smile. I feel the next wave coming and the doctor's faraway voice says, This is it. Time to work. I give it everything. I throw down in the pit. Big heavy rocks and tree limbs are hurtling high and crashing down as I bear down like a Grizzly landing on all fours.

I'm on my back and the doctor's hand is up inside me trying to wrestle out a soft scull. It hurts and I wish she wouldn't do that but I am on a leash, tied down to this cold place until I let out a huge sound and water and blood and an unusually large head all come out in a rushing gush that is immediately a still puddle. The room is all dead stares and silence but I am gone. I start to climb up above everyone. I am traveling back to the midwives and I am relieved to find them still dancing. I join in and hold their hands for now I am one of them. No more baby hanging out, I am free and lighter than air. I am smiling. My work is done.

The corpse inside is laid bare. The nurses wrap her body in a plain blanket and gingerly lay this object in my arms. I can't see her. There is only a brown patch that is supposed to be her face. They told me she might be brown if she had been dead a few days, but it is still shocking. I ask them to unwrap her. I need to see her. Whole. Hoping there is more. But it's nothing. It's not human. It's like jelly or jell-o. Limp. Liquid. Melted. And dark. It's a fake. I am stunned. Like a bitch leaving her deformed puppy to freeze in the cold, I turn away. She is dead now and now we know. She left long ago. Her body has begun to disintegrate. To dissolve back into the nothingness she came from.

If her body was closer to living, I might have missed her. I might have seen something. A resemblance. Might have cried holding her tiny body, still warm with spirit. But this is not the case and I see a blessing. There is nothing here to love. I am off the hook! So I joke that it looks like a cow's liver. No one is laughing but me. So I try another, hoping to lighten the room. I had a baby! Don't you see? She is born, but not into that brown blob! My baby is NOT here. Just this strange brown. That is NOT her. That is what happened to her. Her leftover corpse. They are all sad. Dave is sad. I will have to play sad too. But I feel happy.

After the conversation with the undertaker. After saying goodbye to the body bag. After a night of half sleep. After a kind nurse gives a cold warning that my body will still go through the motions. My milk will arrive and the elation of raging hormones will soon wear off. After we sign papers, they hand me a puffy cream colored box full of institutionally-minded keepsakes, a pamphlet about support-groups, a blurry footprint and two Polaroid's of her body. They make me sick. They make me sit in a wheelchair. They roll me out through the maternity ward where I can feel mountains of bliss and joy, thankfully contained behind closed doors. I feel I am disintegrating, held together by a single loose thread. As they wheel me past the nurse's station, no one looks up. My arms are empty. Instead, I grip the pitiful cream colored box on my lap.

Outside on the pavement, the California sunshine brightens me. We get back in our car. Just yesterday we came here to find out what was wrong. Today we don't recognize ourselves. We are forever changed. My adrenaline high and our combined lack of sleep have made us both feel slightly crazy and we drive home to Eagle Rock, elated and laughing. We stop for coffee. Why not? And while I wait in the car for Dave to come back, a pregnant woman walks past. She is huge. She is due any day and I can smile. The midwives are still dancing around my head like an animated halo, making me feel strong, satisfied, even proud to say I feel no envy. I had my baby. My work is done.

We go home and I sit on the edge of the bed with the cream colored box beside me.

The corpse is laid bare. I try, but I cannot look inside the box. I cannot see what I know at the core to be true. That she is not for this world. That my body's hard work and all our love is not for that child. The corpse laid bare. I must look and I must see. She is part of me. Dead.

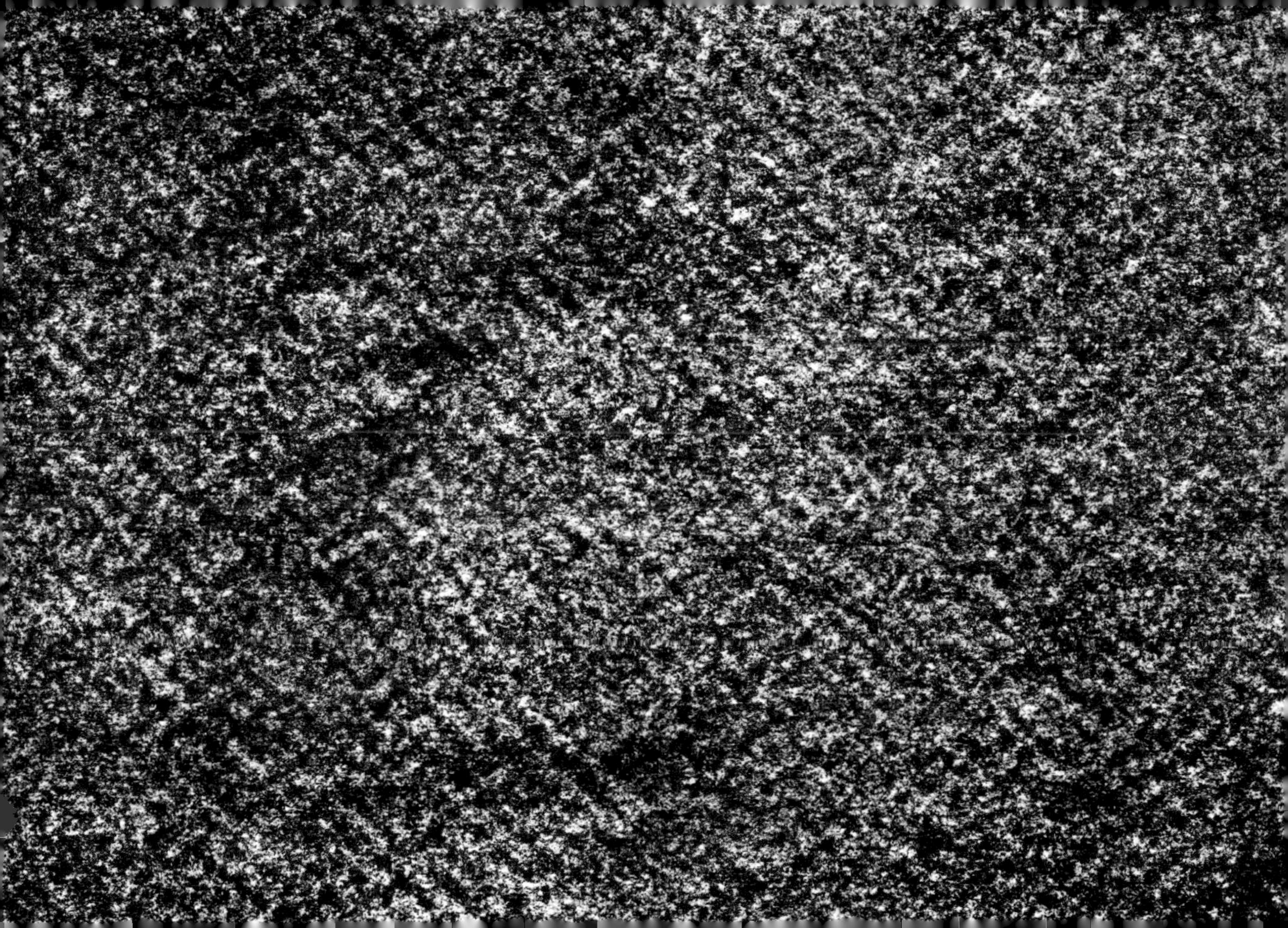

Mermaid

The beautiful blond in the blue mermaid dress has a question
Mommie?
Yes
Can you help me make some tiny diapers for the doll house?
Yes. Bring me the scissors from my black bag in the bathroom, do you know the one?
Yes
And the diaper is on top of the changing table
Ok

She runs to the house and I watch her through the window of my studio
Blond ringlets bouncing down her back

Sunlight sparkling the blue sequins of her gown
Eyes wide with anticipation
Of making tiny diapers

I can take a break from writing to help with her small project
It's more fun and it helps me to stay the inner voice
That ruthlessly criticizes my mothering
You are too wrapped up in yourself
You should be spending more time with your children

The voice is cruel

It is not mine
It is certainly not my mothers
It belongs to someone I heard on the radio years ago
And read in a magazine yesterday
It is the voice of fear
Present in all mothers
But more acute in some
Of failure

One must live with faith
Every day
That the worst may only seem that way at first
That death is not the end
Unless we choose it to be

And beauty is all around us
In the trees and the sky and the tip of a fingernail
And in the cloud of blond curls
Falling down her back

Later she returns
This time in underwear
Tears running down her cheeks
Mommie I hurt myself she says opening the door with an excuse she knows will always get her in
She needs a kiss
And it has to be mine

Butterfly

There is a big yellow and black striped Swallowtail in our garden. We've spotted her many times, and we all noticed her on Grace's birthday, flying around the yard during the party. Grace was excited because she had wanted butterflies on her cake, which she got, made of almond slices. I took a picture of the cake and the swallowtail, as if for proof.

The butterfly is here now. I feel like she wants to be acknowledged, so I watch for a moment or two, until a voice says, Get back to work, and I look back at what I was writing. Another fainter voice says, Look at me, so I look up again, and watch her flutter about the bush. I say out loud, If you want me to see you, why don't you come closer? This is a test. She stays where she is, but opens her wings all the way, turning her body, and the question, to me. I hoist myself out of the hammock and walk over to the bush she is perched on. I am just a foot or two away and I can clearly see the perfection that is hers. The touches of iridescent blue with bits of green in the upper part of her tail and the fine hairs on her large, black body. I can see the texture of her wings, like tiny tissue paper tiles. She stays absolutely still for what seems like a long time, persuading me to revel in her glory. Then she flies up, circles around behind me and disappears.

I had been writing about intuition, about how easy it is to trick myself into ignoring what I can clearly feel, or see. The way I knew there was something wrong when I was pregnant with Keirnan but chose to deny it. I was writing about the yoga teacher who pointed out in front of a whole class that I was very small for being six months pregnant.

She turned out to be right of course because Keirnan was developing slower than normal and by then had all but stopped growing. On some level I must have known the yoga teacher was right and so her comment made me very angry. How dare she say such a thing? But had there been no fear, I don't think I would have cared.

I took the swallowtail's timing as a sign, to trust the inner voice more. She started hanging around right about the same time that I began to feel a presence, the way I did with Grace. Dave has noticed her too as he passes through the back yard many times a day going to his studio, and agrees that she seemed to represent something. I am feeling brave enough to picture this butterfly as another child, waiting to become part of my body, and our family. And a voice says, Why not?

Trying

The night Keirnan was born, the doctor told us not to wait too long before trying again. She reminded me of my age and said we had to wait three months, but after that we should start. I looked at my midwife, Margo, who was sitting back in the corner of the room. She lifted one eyebrow as if to say, Let's talk about this when we're alone.

A few days later Margo came to visit me at home and we did. She said she had seen people try again too early and it never worked out. Wait at least six months, but nine would be better, she said. I knew absolutely that she was right. But there was a part of me, very strong, that wanted her to be wrong and was eager to start trying as soon as possible.

At six months, I was almost feeling whole. I convinced myself we were good to go and

Dave went a long with my enthusiasm. I shared the doctor's concern about my age, and even though she assured me Keirnan's deformity had nothing to do with it, I could not help but feel my chances of having a healthy baby were dwindling with each passing month.

Grace and Keirnan were both conceived on the first try. But now my period came like clockwork, eating away my confidence each month as it rolled in like the tide. Seeing that bit of blood would ruin the day.

Dave kept reminding me that things would work out. He wouldn't let me get caught in games of timing it or looking for signs that I was ovulating. He wasn't interested in over thinking the process and had little patience for me when I tried to.

The last time I had one of those disappointing days was Christmas. I had been full of hope that morning. We were visiting Dave's family up North and I ran to the bathroom just as we were about to open presents. There it was. The red menace I had come to despise. Thanks a lot, I said looking up. Merry Christmas.

In January my period didn't come on time, but I waited to do a pregnancy test. I didn't want to get my hopes up and Keirnan's birthday was just around the corner. So on her birthday, a week late for my period, I went to the drug store to get the test. I walked in through the automatic glass doors finally letting myself believe I was pregnant again. I felt sure handing my money to the cashier and she smiled at me. I went home and happily peed on the little white stick. I looked up and said Thank you, this time sincerely, before running in to tell Dave.

Bad Dream

A baby boy is born. It is dark and there are people everywhere. In the dream I am at a party or a fundraiser or some large gathering. It is crowded. I am distracted by all the people, the noise. It dawns on me that I am free. Free from the burden of pregnancy. Free to talk to people, to show myself to the world again. My body is back to being flat. Breasts are empty. Wait, my breasts are empty? A terrifying realization rushes through me. I forgot to nurse my baby. I forgot to feed him. It has been hours or maybe days and I forgot about him. How could I? Frantically I search rooms to see where I left him and find him on a bed, dead. He is dark and limp and gone because I forgot about him. He is not coming back.

I begin to wail. I am walking and wailing and everyone sees me and knows why. The people in this place are my friends. They give me space. Almost like they expected it. It feels like they are thinking, We knew this one would end badly. We knew you would not be able to have another baby. I am walking and wailing as hard as I can. I don't care anymore. I will wail until I die. I will not stop. There is no reason to stop.

I woke up crying, unable to stop, then not wanting to. I got up and moved into the living room, afraid of waking Dave. But he followed and found me crouched in a ball on the couch. I cried for a long time in his arms. We were on the couch that is really a bed with wedge shaped pillows and I was staring at the dark green bedspread we bought at Ikea before all this happened.

The next day I cried on and off all day. It was one of those fragile vulnerable days when I feel like I am barely holding on. I knew the dream was about fear and I felt shaken, but also cleansed and rejuvenated. The day after I felt amazing. Elated. Confident that the baby is fine. She is moving a lot.

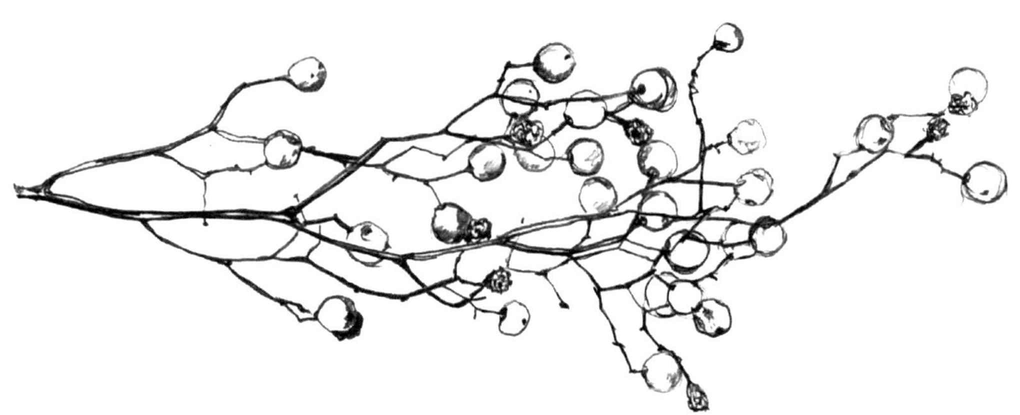

Home Birth

I was so grateful to be pregnant with Frances that I relished it in a way I had not with Grace or Keirnan. But the pregnancy was also clouded with plenty of fear. The fear would show itself in dreams mostly, but there were also irrational thoughts throughout the day that I would have to ignore or discard. Some people were concerned about our choice to have Frances at home. They considered it brave after Keirnan. But I felt proud of both previous births. My body knew exactly what to do, my labors were not long and I managed pain well. I love childbirth and I trusted my midwife Margo completely. I had no desire to be in a hospital for this one, and I knew deep down that Frances was fine. I was finding a lot of feathers on my walks and I took each one as a sign that things would be okay.

Dave was also confident. Just being in his presence makes me feel safe, so when he is sure of something, it helps a lot. I woke him up at two in the morning to say I was in labor, and a huge grin took over his broad face.

Frances took her time being born. Margo and I were both under the impression she would come as fast as Grace and Keirnan had, but after laboring for about six hours I had to take a walk around the block to get her going. It was dawn and Dave and Grace came with me. Every few steps I would lean on Dave while I had a contraction and I might as well have been leaning on one of the massive Oaks that line our street. Grace followed us, nervous and talkative. When we finally got home, Frances seemed ready to come out. But she was like a snail, slowly poking her feelers out into the world to see if it was safe. After pushing hard for about twenty minutes, her head came and Margo told me I had to push again for her shoulders, and then again for her hips. Dave had to pull her the rest of the way. I wasn't expecting her to be so beautiful. Or my vanishing fear to be so palpable as it lifted off my shoulders. I felt I might float off the bed as I held her wet body in my arms and thanked her for coming.

I passed out on the way to the bathroom a little while later. I collapsed in Margo's arms. When I came to there was a circle of concerned faces above me. They were completely unfamiliar at first. Then I recognized them slowly, one at a time. First Grace, then Dave, then Margo.

New Mother

I am sitting on a lounge chair in the desert. There's a computer on my lap and headphones over my ears. I am trying to write about her again, finally. I am struggling a bit but it is beginning to flow. My fingers tapping fast. Then I pause to think of a word and a piece of music starts that stops everything. The strings sweep me out of my head, pushing me to look over the top of the computer screen at the landscape turning blue right in front of me. I almost missed this, I think and suddenly a familiar sadness settles in. I miss my mother.

I am poised to indulge in the soft comfort of old grief but instead I wait. And in that tiny opening a voice says, There is something better to do with this. Stay with it. Enjoy the changing colors. I close my eyes and open my hands and fall in. It is a choice, like any other. I can always find this place and acknowledge that this is her love. It is not to be missed, it is to be felt. Fill up with it. I am sitting with her in the balcony of the concert hall listening to this piece of music. And I can love her for who she is and where she is. She is all around me always. In my tears and my lungs and my fingers on the keyboard.

Another Dream

A baby lies at the bottom of the bathtub
Murky water obscures the fine details
Wisps of brown hair
Glistening skin
Tiny fingernails

I wake up from the dream to the nervous ticking of a clock. Frances has been sleeping for more than two hours. I quickly go in to check on her. She is up on all fours and smiling. I lift her, drinking up her hair and her drool, swallowing her milky breath.

Birthday

We are walking across an expanse of grass in a park we've never visited before. Grace is holding my hand and Frances is riding my hip. Sponge Bob, Spider Man and a purple dinosaur are bobbing at the other end of the field, marking distinct birthday parties. I think it's the Spider Man, Grace offers without prompting. Nathan loves Spider Man.

Nathan's mother is coming toward us. She is waving a big smile. Hello! I'm so glad you came, she says emphatically and guides us to the picnic tables she has staked out. Nathan is a friend from Grace's small preschool, but we've never socialized with him outside of class before. The invitation was unexpected and we made a Herculean effort to get here.

We sit down at the benches and I am glad to see Nancy, another mom from Grace's class. She is the only one I've had more than just passing interactions with. We talk about the summer and her older daughter who is already a teenager. It appears that the rest of the forty or so guests are family. Grace sits down behind me with a handful of chips and starts talking to a girl who is twice her size and looks more than twice her age. Grace loves older girls and is good at keeping them interested in talking to her.
I am half eavesdropping on their conversation, the way I do when I don't know the person Grace is talking to, just as a precaution. Grace is precocious in her speech and sometimes can get in over her head. Grace asks if she is Nathan's sister and the girl laughs. She says they are just cousins and that she is one of four girls. She asks Grace if Frances is her only sister and Grace answers no. I have another sister, but she is up in

the sky. Up in the sky is a term we use for anyone who is dead. My mother is up in the sky, Uncle Jack is up in the sky, Jane the cat and the pigeon we found in the driveway last week are both up in the sky. It is not a euphemism. Grace might just as easily have said she had a sister who died or was still born. She uses the language around mortality that adults often stumble over without hesitation. It is normal for us to talk about Keirnan and death. The conversations are a reach into the unknown for all of us, and she has led us through them more often than not. I never give her pat answers about life's great mysteries. I enjoy letting the words *No one knows* be the answer.

The older girl says she has a younger sister who died too. She isn't sure how old she was when it happened or what her sister's name was. We never talk about her, she says very matter of fact without a hint of regret. I manage to hold back from inserting myself in their exchange. Then Grace pipes, Well we do, adding with glee, We celebrate her birthday!

Another Storm

This one announces itself with a loud crack while I am meditating. As I open my eyes I watch the sky darken and head downstairs for my camera. We are on vacation in Vermont. Out on the dock ominous black and blue clouds are moving in accompanied by low rumbles. The light is slipping through in places making sharp curtains of yellow that hang from the low clouds to the surface of the water. I snap pictures, excited to add this drama to a series I have started of the lake. Darkness comes quickly and the curtains evaporate. I hear the distinct patter of rain drops on the water moments before I see them coming. The drops are bouncing and shimmering in a way that it hard to believe. I've watched it rain on this lake countless times but I've never seen this show before. Without thinking I start to run inside for shelter but stop myself, turn around and take more pictures instead.

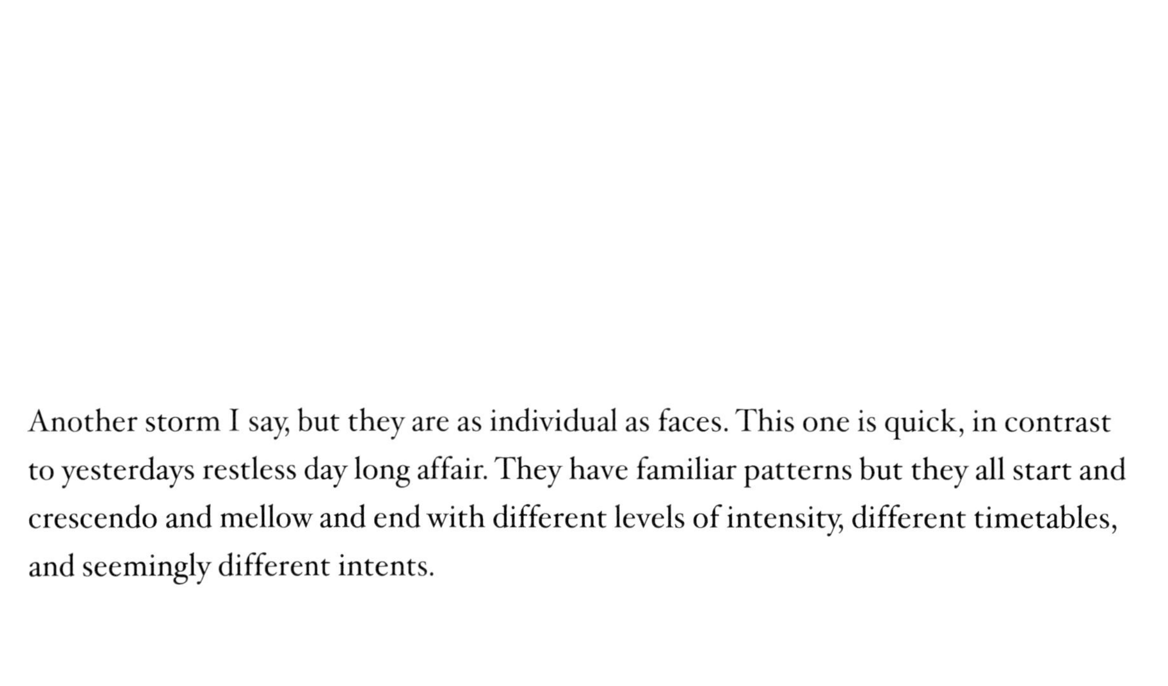

Another storm I say, but they are as individual as faces. This one is quick, in contrast to yesterdays restless day long affair. They have familiar patterns but they all start and crescendo and mellow and end with different levels of intensity, different timetables, and seemingly different intents.

All Gone

No more booby I say
Bye-bye booby
Booby all gone

Her face is swollen
Red and wet
She can barely look at me

She rides my hip
Waiting for her time
For old times sake

She gets mad
She waddles into the pantry, pulling
food from the shelves
she dumps it on the floor

These are her words

She's leaving in the arms of her babysitter
Trying to be brave and wave
But today she is not cheerful

She reaches for me
Real sad in her
And I take her back

Her big head on my shoulder
My arm is her seat
In her back, a sigh lifts and
settles

The Return

Resistance has been my companion
Ever since we got back
Resistance to meditating and writing
I'd rather busy myself with laundry
Sorting, hanging and folding brightly colored cloth
Chopping onions and placing them in a bowl
Pulling the dress over the little head and getting a smile in return
Running the yarn over and around and through with the needle,
pinching and pulling it into something satisfying
I avoid the mail
Letting it lie on the floor where the mail shoot drops it

The persistent dreams of Frances drowning
The feeling I know what's coming and it's not good
I carry this around
It came up today in my breath
I pulled a card for comfort
And got the whale
And it sang to me
A song of deep sadness
As though the one I've been holding
was never mine at all

Puppet Show

Frances sits on my lap during the performance. The barn is warm with bodies that crowd the bleachers. We are in the very back, the top row of wooden seats. She can barely see over the shoulders in front of us but she is entranced by the sight of people in costumes, dancing animals, and the musicians who are on a balcony above the stage, across the air from us.

She sits facing forward, quiet and content for the first half of the show. As boredom begins to make her restless she turns to me, making faces, pressing her lips to my glasses, pulling away again and making more faces. She's succeeding at making me laugh. She leans her head on my shoulder and pats me on the back saying mamamamama.

Now she wants to stand on my lap and her sturdy little feet balance on the soft muscles of my thighs which move this way and that. I have to hold her hips to keep her there but we are comfortable this way. She leans her body against my shoulder and I rest my head against her doughy side. Through the gummy dank of the barn, I can still find her milky smell. For now, we are complete in ourselves and as one. But not for long. Soon she is squirming, unable to settle back in with me. She is tired and getting angry and there is no amount of cajoling that will shift her now. I lift her and stand with effort, all too aware that soon she will outgrow my lap for good.

Dead Birds

At a friend's house
One appeared
Inexplicably, no sound
Just suddenly there on the ground

One of the little girls saw it first
But I recognized it
As mine

The first ones were brutal
Tiny dead babies

Next to broken shells
On my doorstep

I would ask God what kind of cruel joke he thought he was playing
I would ask Dave to dispose of them
A proper burial beyond me

Later there was the parrot
Which Grace and I tried to revive
And then the pigeon who I greeted as more of a sign
But still unsure of what

Then of course the baby crow
Memorialized in its own poem
And seen as a gift

This one, like the others, is at first mysterious
I watch as my friend
Calmly but quickly buries it
Among the leafy plants in her garden

She replies to a string of questions from the girls
in a sing song voice with short answers
that don't satisfy

Is it dead? Is it hurt? Will it wake up? What happened?
Will it be okay? Does it want to be buried? Why did it die?

When the answers are curt
When there is the hint of a cover up, a secret
curiosity grows deep
Especially when they sense their right to know

I notice with pride
That is probably silly but nonetheless mine
That Grace is not asking any questions

And the string of dead birds
Makes a parallel arc
Beginning with the brutal truth
That death has a right to us

Ending with simple comforts
That life continues in cycles
Heals with its rhythmic flowering
Of inevitable beauty

Keirnan

Just moments after she was born I said, I think we should give her the name. Dave's eyes were already filled with tears and now his chest began to heave. The grief pushed up and out of him like a volcano. Dave is a big man, and to see him cry is startling and beautiful. He knew what I meant. The name was Keirnan and he had picked it. I could see him, a couple of months earlier, announcing it to me in the bathroom as he dried himself with a towel. I agreed immediately. It was unusual and pretty. I could tell he was proud of having thought of it.

I think he felt sad giving it to a dead baby, as if it would be wasted. I felt there was no choice. It was the only name we had and it already seemed to belong to her.

Ironically, the name was anything but buried. It became the working title of this book, and both of us used it in some form for various passwords. When we talk about her, we always use her name. We rarely say the still birth, or the baby that died, because those are harder to say. And they don't allow for her to exist anymore, which she does. So it is very much in use. I don't say it aloud fifty times a day like I do Grace and Frances, so it still has a special feeling around it. It is like a name that has been thought of but not yet given, even though it has.

Last day

Last chance to finish up the drawing
that became the epic
How to draw
the view of the lake
the trees across it
the branches that frame it
impossible seeming
nonetheless attempted
shows promise
is continued
loose here, tight there
almost finished
never done